Maggie Rigg

Spillweir

A Collection of Poems in support of
Cerebral Palsy Plus

ISBN: 978-0-244-98382-6

Copyright © 2018 by Maggie Rigg

All rights reserved. This book or any portion thereof may not be reproduced or used in any manner whatsoever without the express written permission of the publisher.

First Printing: 2018

Publisher: M. Rigg et al

Cover designed by Badger

Acknowledgements

I am grateful to my grandson who inspired me to write these poems and to my daughter for her enthusiasm for me to complete the collection. Also to my grandson's father for his supportive comments. My thanks go to the tutors on many creative writing courses I have attended over the years, members of a creative writing group I currently attend who have contributed constructively to many of the poems, and to Christine Rouse, Dawn Thomson, Rosalie Alston and Zena Butterfield who gave of their time to read through to offer further feedback and comments. To Colin Brown at Poetry Can, Bristol who critiqued the poems and gave me the confidence to move forward to this point. And finally to my sisters Dorothy and Pearl for listening and my brother Dennis, who kindly agreed to proofread the collection.

Introduction

Each year there may be as many as 1,800 children in the UK born with cerebral palsy. This equates to 1 in 400. My grandson is one of them. Each child/adult with cerebral palsy is unique and has a differing range of abilities and an inimitable story to tell. This set of poems offers a glimpse into the first eleven years of my grandson's life. Prompted to write by the hurdles faced, and in some cases overcome, I have tried to give a balanced view of his journey to date, and many of the poems are celebratory.

The collection also includes poems to illustrate the way society can make life more difficult for people with an impairment. The poem *This Space is Reserved for a Wheelchair* was written prior to the bus company being taken to the supreme court in 2017 by a disabled man. Since then I have experienced improved disabled access on the buses.

*These poems are dedicated to
my Grandson A F R
a boy with determination and spirit*

Contents

13	Dawn Journey
14	Afterbirth
15	The Festive Season
16	Sleep Stealer
17	More in Love
18	One Opinion
19	Spillweir
20	Welcome to their World
21	Separation
22	Buttons, Tubes and Knots
23	Map Reading
24	That Summer Holiday
25	Drills
26	A Shed of his Own
27	A Souvenir
28	Freedom
29	Cappuccino
30	At the Grey Metal Gate
31	A Young Apprentice
32	Spillweir 2
33	After the Drowning
34	New Growth
35	Hush
36	Crate Climber
37	Neptune
38	Rolling
39	A Special School
40	When My Daughter was Away
41	The Ming Vase and the Boy in the Power Chair
42	Code Breaking

Contents continued

43	Giving the School-boy a Voice
44	In a Queue
45	A Thank You
46	Spillweir 3
47	What's 'e Got Then?
48	Test Dose
49	The Implant
50	Wilful
51	A Photograph of Camp
52	Walk-through Theatre
53	Speaking of Gardens
54	In the Middle of the Night
55	The Ofsted Inspector
56	Logs and Leaf Mould
57	Harmonious
58	Balloon in the Breeze
59	What Really Gets to Me
60	Spillweir 4
61	Optimism
62	We Sing
63	Our Winner
64	Festival-goer
69	The Head of Play Parks
70	Paralympics July 2012
71	An Inconvenience
72	This Space is Reserved for a Wheelchair
73	A Prayer
74	Swimming Pool Blues
75	Speaking Out

Dawn Journey

Warrior chants and yowls
leapt out of her mouth
like Bolshoi ballerinas,
hushed the hoot of the owl,
the hum of the full moon.

Silence slept.
The dawn chorus eavesdropped
whilst he traversed channel and curve
until, when darkness ended its shift,
he emerged into day-break's wide grin

trailed ruby ribbons along the shore,
where the first sound-waves of adoration
filled the air,
and with his first cry
a new family was born.

Afterbirth

Around the lips of a pond of silence
the expert stood, determined as a nettle
about to rub against a rambler's bare calf

to measure their new-born's downy head
marbled with his mother's precious blood.

His water scorpion-statement *What's been going on,
didn't you know there was something wrong?*
threw accusations at the song of her tenderness

raw from the labour pains of birth.
They wondered what was meant
so they looked down to the earth,

and again to the pool,
but could only see more water scorpions,
pond skaters, no-one who would tell them the truth.

The Festive Season

A carnival, festooned with garlands
of blue, white
a float of baby paraphernalia
of emotions soaring high
in the big-wheel of a new-born.

The non-routine tests
the specialist's concern
forgotten,
hidden beneath
seats of delight. His intakes of breath

drew in family, friends
around his brand-new cot
whilst he napped
through the merriments,
muscles tight as wet rope knots.

Sleep-stealer

Through the dark hours
when he stole our sleep,
moonlight befriended us,
a guide towards our restless gift

dreams for his future buried deep
under worry-wrinkled sheets.
We nursed our baby along with our fears,
sang lullabies, watched

his perfectly formed body
loosen on the journey into
his own sleep's lairs
only to re-awaken seconds later

by the slightest brush
against the flesh arm-rest
the tick of the hours
the flicker of sun-rise.

More in Love

Then came the disruption
the feeding routine
defined by volcanic explosions
of food he'd just eaten.

His head nodded, a glove puppet
in need of a hand,
pounded our shoulders
as we held him tight

aware there was something amiss,
the milestones, indicators
for babies or toddlers
were unhelpful, dismissed.

One Opinion

We kept our appointment along with our giggling
nine-month-old who looked forward to a treat,
instead, we were about to see the consultant

with feet up on the table, an imitation of an illustration
in a children's book, about to step through the pop-up pages
to tell a joke to us.

This informality as he delivered his opinion
gave us false hope when he announced
our child was *Like a broken engine.*

The news was as hard to grasp as algebraic formulae
the heart-losing-blood sensation
of something precious taken.

Being forced to run forward with
the malignant cells of an imprecise diagnosis,
anxiety and optimism ran together, as though they were

children who ran a three-legged race. We rejoiced
at his capabilities, at other times a fog wrapped around us
as it drifted in from inexplicable places.

Spillweir

A lively stream, it ebbed around us
as we crossed one stepping stone of emotion to another,
until balanced riskily

on the lips of the experts, the words *cerebral palsy*
in bold heavy font were spat out.
Once we knew

our anxiety broke through the glass carpet
we had cautiously trodden, in an out of control spin
it surged down from the brim,

a spout into the spiral-gurgle of the spillweir
in torrents,
to clear any doubts.

Welcome to Their World

There came the wise-men and women carrying gifts,
a procession of advice and knowledge marched
into their lives.

It forced them to make room for long-term
uninvited guests who brought a hybrid
of the delicately wrapped and valued

blended with opinions that stuck like tar to shoes,
rested under finger-nails, impossible to remove.

Professionals' guidance became routine,
at times as unwelcome as hair frizzing in the rain,
but once his parents realised that they themselves

were the experts of their child they shut the doors,
changed the locks, to claim their privacy once again.

Separation

We felt the sharp sting when the nurse
plunged the cannula into the back of your hand,
heard your loud bawl,

the crust of disbelief across your ashen face
that of a child who has not won a giant teddy
at a fairground stall.

We tried to hold it together, stay calm.
Any doubts were put to one side
when we recalled the torturous mealtimes, your distress,

the last leftovers of patience scraped from our plates.
We believed the decisions reached were for the best
and although a premature separation felt severe

we were hopeful of the operation's success
to transform you from a coughing and jetting coffee machine
into a smoothie, a fair exchange.

Buttons, Tubes and Knots

With all these in place
dessert and main
became a past pleasure
nil by mouth the norm

banana flavoured sustenance
pumped through a tube
minute by minute
his replacement routine

to leave taste buds redundant
no chocolates, savouries or sweets
only a frequent taste ascended
from his stomach as it released

the pleasure of a flavour
of what he now missed.

Map Reading

She unrolled her determination like
A-roads on a map. Without directions she drove forward
to fight for his rights, never deterred by cul-de-sacs

or slippery paths. In all weathers she followed the
signs at crossroads, trailed down tracks to find solutions.
She navigated through dark tunnels,

bridges, avenues lined with branches to cling to,
bounties of solutions to select.
At every roundabout she reduced her speed

checked each exit, searched for rare-rocks
of information, scraps of wisdom
a perpetual passage of spirit, optimism.

That Summer Holiday

That day
that moment sand sieved through our toes
that sea ironed smooth as glass
that phone call, a jolt into another world
that one we'd left behind
that voice pitched as though a car was breaking speed
that came from someone unqualified to say
that he was more brain damaged than first believed
that she told us whilst on holiday
that shock like snake fangs in the flesh

that letter of complaint
that unsatisfactory response
that meeting when she denied her big mistake
that no-one had complained before
that smirk upon her face
that lump which rested in our throats
that bitter biro-ink aftertaste.

Drills

They pulled and stretched
stretched and pulled him
into frog-like positions.
His cries
created tightened muscles
stiff arms, stiff legs
holding on to his body's
classified intelligence.
They told us he would have to
get used to this daily routine
no excuses
no more tearful scenes.

A Shed of his Own

As a two-year-old in the nursery class
he sat propped against a bean bag,
his hair a bubble bath of blonde curls,
giggle as infectious as a yawn.

The attentive staff tried to work him out,
as though they were a group of cavers
finding their way through a maze of
undiscovered chambers and halls.

Only the dolls he befriended knew his
secrets, that he teased the grown-ups
about knowing all his colours except red.

He told them too about his own shed
at the bottom of the playground to park his
buggy, because he was worth it.

A Souvenir

When he had been lifted into an adapted ski-chair
to the zenith of the mountain, we drank hot mulled wine
to numb our trepidation at his ascent,

afterwards his unscathed downward spiral.
We waited, watched as the double-feet
stitched through the satin white fabric

magnified breath by frozen breath, until the green
of his ski suit ripped down the slope
and whooshed to a halt.

.

Freedom

Rolling in, it resembled a Henry Hoover
with its red robust body, wide-eyed expression.
At first the small boy bottom-lipped

uneasy about being seated on its lap or pressing
the electronic arm lights. His fear and his form
rendered his body timber-tight until a cautious confidence

relaxed him into its seat. When he realised his power
he drove fast forward, revved into reverse.
Gaining momentum, he spiralled a pathway

through the safety of his playroom,
showed off to the now anxious audience
his newly-found freedom.

Cappuccino

The froth on the surface
embraces the sprinkled
cocoa reserved for him,
spoon after spoon
of carefully skimmed optimism.

A ritual, greedy traces of
chocolate smear cheeks and lips
face paint
a giveaway to his thirst
for the lukewarm creamy taste

flavoured with melt in the mouth
fine bubbles of coffee, a rush of
anticipation, delight,
of promises of more to come
for our eager child.

At the Grey Metal Gate

He stared and they in turn eyed back.
They had no commitment to their long days or nights
other than to eat, shuffle and bray.

Their monotone hee-haws startled.
Whilst the clock's hands circled, like team members
in a rounder's match, past ten, then coffee time

he sat mesmerized.
In the meantime, other youngsters came and went
from the grey metal gate; little pop-up children.

The nine creatures hypnotized him
his affinity with them palpable
but I had forgotten to bring a magazine.

A Young Apprentice

After a three-year apprenticeship
he was able to complete the job
to a standard ready to be trusted.

Watch as he takes the flat stick
between thumb and forefinger,
steadies the weight pointing upwards,
the tongue-shaped ice at the tip.

Mouth open wide, he tastes the
strawberry and orange flavours,
a watercolour sunset
down his chin, his chest.

The stick slips from time to time
from twelve to quarter past
but he shows determination
to complete the demanding task.

Spillweir 2

The pair were brim-full with strain when passion,
clothed in funereal black, flirted with the spillweir
before it overflowed, a runaway.

Affection followed as it dived into the subterranean
to gush along with other deceased emotions,
its powerful surges drowned relationship's memoir.

All that remained was the occasional warmth
of the thistledown beside the feathers of their life together,
debris afloat on the surface

along with heartache, love's sorrow.

After the Drowning

Sadness hovered, a ghost over the spillweir's surface.
Some days it grabbed his hand,
squeezed it hard to confuse or console

at other times drifted away to a place
where it lay, a dormouse in hibernation.
He would tell us without speech,

now and again an expression of grief
finger to his chin, bottom lip rested tightly over his top lip,
a firmly sealed envelope. His eyes looked for reassurance

in a smile, a glance, hopeful his parent's love
wouldn't change, that all would be okay,
that he was blameless.

New Growth

After the separation smoulder turned to cooled cinders
a bee sting sensation lingered until love's salve
worked its miracle, when, along with the first

snowdrops, he opened up to acceptance,
later variations in the family tree with new branches,
fresh leaves and in the autumn healthier fruits.

Throughout the seasons, he breathed in
the constant-caress of each parent's devotion
an affirmation the family he created with his first cry

remained his closest kinsfolk.

Hush

When you told the experts he could say
Hello and *Oh dear* they raised their eyebrows,
blinked with incredulity,
were as silent as a cold cup of tea.

When you mentioned he could direct his way home
faster than a helter-skelter
by pointing this way and that
they were absent as cuckoos in winter.

When you fought for him to attend mainstream school
they were as mute as sleepy owls
sceptical he understood every word
every vowel.

When accepted at the school of your choice
and told everyone the news and were excited
that your words had finally been heard,
they were as quiet as a deserted classroom.

At the school where he is accepted
nothing exempted
those who were silent with disbelief
are now hushed as a broken whistle.

Crate Climber

His silhouette moves upwards
towards the summer solstice sky
slow as idleness
safety helmet caught by the light

as though a second sun has appeared.
two actors dodging
between the flickers of bottle green.

Suspended on the end of a crane pulley
he is almost out of sight
tucked between the shade of the canopy
the forest giants

where he dangles spellbound in a harness
crates stacked underneath
twelve or thirteen high.

Neptune

He floats with
the sharks
dolphins
pufferfish
the electric eel
mermaids
seahorses.

He is nine-years-old
the spirit of water.
Watch as he
kicks and splashes
with confidence
zeal.
In the water he is
Neptune's
son of the sea.

Rolling

For our child, tunnels of silver steel robots
make sliding confined. Ropes lure,
boys and girls pegged by fingers
clamber and hang, washing on a line.

Basket-swings full of children's rosy cheeks
resemble freshly hatched eggs
as they kick, shriek.
Skate boards flip their giant game of Tiddlywinks.

Wheels scrape,
but for him it is an almost barren scene
apart from the grassy hillocks he rolls down
at least ten times, sometimes fifteen.

A Special School

The experts argued with the force of politicians
that he should attend a *special school*.
This became a challenge,

but we found one where the children are not
segregated into goldfish bowl classrooms
or identified by disability or diligence.

One where all children are welcomed,
stirred like eggs into a cake, sweet jam
spread in the middle of a Victoria sponge.

Children are wheeled around by able-bodied peers,
basic sign language is a familiar exchange.
Every child is nurtured,

their names voiced with affection
around each teacher's tongue, and our boy is excited
at the start of every school day.

This school is *special*.

When my Daughter was Away

On a hot under the soles of sandals afternoon
I bravely encouraged my grandson to sail.
Hoisted as though a shipping container,

packed tightly to avoid a slip, a slide, or perishing
his expression of resignation and trust
non-identical twins,

a reminder that I was his protector
precariously so, even though
a skilled yachtsman took the lines.

I watched as he vanished into the sole of the small vessel
and prayed to whoever listens to non-believers,
an invocation to sail back safely

in the origami replica, ebbing away
into my incubus of a lost-at-sea boy; and my daughter,
what would she do, what would she say?

The Ming Vase and the Boy in the Power Chair

Placed on a pedestal in the museum's small room
the fourteenth-century vessel boasted its splendour,
under the spotlight's glare it shone out in the gloom.

The curator, his job dependent on its protection,
guarded it with anxious authority
a family member's affection.

Meanwhile as he circumnavigated the museum's corridors
in his new powered chair, the boy chose
the 'tortoise' button on its electronic device,

until he entered the room of the museum's special piece,
I closed my eyes nervous of what might happen next
(China's history cascading like beads from a broken necklace?)

He stared at the exhibit with mischievous delight
then without a second's delay pressed the 'hare' button,
and aimed straight for the ancient artefact.

Code Breaking

When we fill the air
with our whispers
of treats
sleepovers
he listens, a fine harpist
as he plucks out the relevant vowels
consonants
the mumble of conspiracy
the shushes and silences between
until
he recognises the tune
guesses the surprise
the treat
sometimes even before
we open our jaw
or the first resonance leaves our lips.

Giving the School-boy a Voice

In year one, the first power of speech given
was electronic, a man's. Its sounds resembled
a vintage wireless when played
across long to medium wave bands.

His use of it laborious with random words,
songs and letters often a senseless jabber.
Some years later the voice, a boy's,
conveyed expressive chatter into his efforts

at sentence building; asking for a cappuccino,
spelling out the word *delicious*
as he spooned the chocolatey froth from its surface
or said *Thank you* to show his politeness.

In a Queue

All twenty-six are jumbled
they struggle to sort themselves
into words
in the rush to get out
as they force their way
through the tangled conduits.

A few queue jump
and like baby sea turtles
in their race to the ocean
some succeed
others never quite make it
but those that do slip through the tongue
delight the listener.

A Thank You

To the drums for the feel of the sticks on stretched skin
awakened into an off-key rhythm. The chimes with
their long silver tubes encourage you to run your fingers
along their scales, to delight at their tune.

The shakers that imitate rain-on-the-roof,
the piano with its chink-chink as your fingers stumble
across white teeth, the therapist who sings, but leaves gaps
for you to fill in with any sounds you want, to incite
pandemonium.

The range of the instruments, the welcome tribute,
the way you change your mind as you try to blow through the
flute. The warmth in their faces gives you a comfortable space
in which to make choices, at your own pace.

Spillweir 3 (House Adaptions)

The foundations were the toughest part;
doors opened, then unexpectedly slammed shut in her face,
the emotional breeze blocks
grey, heavy forced her down

into the engulfing channels of the overspill
but being a strong swimmer
her desire to move forward with rapidity
drove her over every ripple, every swell

towards new designs, skilled help. Her pulse regained
strength enough to offer splashes of motivation,
an occasional harsh wave at the too narrow,
the badly built, or not to plan,

but she never lost faith in the visioned outcome.
Her energy, her determination proved to be the buttress
that filtered through to safeguard a home
to meet his growing needs.

What's 'e Got Then?

If you follow us on our travels
you will notice us being waylaid
by passers-by who rummage,
as though for bargains at a Boxing day sale
and think it's okay to ask us,
What's 'e got then?

When we give them our reply
that he has two parents who love him,
a family who care and protect
they look quizzical, stare,
at an answer
they least expect.

Test Dose

The procedure complete, he lay
body empty of tiger muscle
eyelids heavy as though
overweight fairies slept on his lashes.
Hands flopped like a dangle

of mittens from the sleeves of a child's coat.
From his mouth came whimpers
a plea to feel well again.
When we told the blue cotton-robed
that he was slow to recover

they removed the cannula
pumping the B-drug into his spinal cord
then told us,
the test dose had been successful.

The Implant

With the bulk of a metal tape measure,
the implant was to rest under his skin
near his belt-line at the front of his boy-body.
The stainless steel bullet-proof implant placed to release

the B-drug one miniscule drop by miniscule drop daily
into his skeletal muscles was to assist them to loosen up
like WD40 on a rusty lock. Or might it aggravate
to stop his inclination to rough-roll down knolls

and sand dunes, to cavort in the enjoyable
water play, or be a torturous nuisance,
like being forced to wear a tight woolly jumper?
The judgement weighed heavily on them.

Wilful

He will not wear his coat
(except without a fuss),
long sleeved pyjamas,
a vest, mittens or the tee shirt
with the neck that pulls tight
over his head
or isn't buttoned up.

He will not wear his socks
up high near his knees,
definitely not in wrinkles
but smooth around his ankles, please.
His glasses must be smudge free
or he will cry out to have them cleaned
immediately!

He is wilful, and we are pleased.

A Photograph of Camp

They stand together, an earth of bright-eyed fox cubs
in a self-made den of gathered branches
from the forest's floor

you smile out at what has been achieved,
anticipatory of what is yet to come.
Sitting at the front expectant
the camera captures you happy

in this school camp, where you feel the excitement
of a sleepover with your peers
who accept your differences.

This realisation makes us content too,
though we know we cannot always hold
this level of elation.

Walk-through Theatre

We trail through tunnels
of carbon blackness
flesh touches
bones to shift pebbles, boulders
towards the pop-up pictures
of his future.

An audience at the front
unable to predict how the story
we try to fathom will unfold.
We shadow each other
in the darkness

where we move
without voice or script
never able to predict what's in store
until the safety curtain lowers.
An interlude
in which to focus one day at a time.

Speaking of Gardens

See how his garden grows,
beyond the boundaries of the backyard,
the warm-hearted hot-tub's pummelling,
the night sky where he tallies-up its jewels
to the rhythmic yap of a dog's bark.

His garden meanders onto the virgin grass
where he rolls, unravels energetic giggles,
wanders into woodland to gather earthy souvenirs,
rides along paths overhung with luminous boughs,
a guide into warrens and dens.

It is his vast orchard where
throughout his seasons
the yield is abundant in adventures,
friendship, wisdom, challenge, tenderness, love.
This is his garden.

In the Middle of the Night

When I cannot sleep because next to me a dragon
puffs clouds of chimeras across my pillow,
teases the rhythm of my heart, pounding

at my notions of how I would carry him out
should my house breathe flames too big for me to smother
with a cushion or to quench with a bowl of water,
a soaked towel.

I work out my route but am prevented by the mouth
of heat and smoke which I must overcome to rescue him
where he sleeps at the back of the house.

Restless, frantic, wide awake I unplug his night feed,
take out his line to stop it catching on my escape plot,
open the window just wide enough for us to leave,

bundle him inside the duvet cover somehow,
try to lower him to safety out of the window
but he is too heavy. My plan is severely flawed.

The Ofsted Inspector

Her determined handshake asserted
the battle she'd won for a place
in the only school to embrace his requirements,
the oxygen

to succeed in his own time
without pressure to compare or compete,
to trust that the attainable will be achieved
this year or next.

An adaptable approach
for children whose necessity for support
and integration is uppermost.

Aids to communicate, doors open wide
for children with diverse needs,
those others besides.

It was her moment to sing
which she took with satisfaction
a merit of *Outstanding* her conclusive opinion.

Logs and Leaf Mould

His baby curls fall away
like spring flower petals under April showers
the boy in the mirror uses his fingers to comb out the years.

He ruffles his hair into a stylish spikey affair
to match his cheeky, sideways-shy glance
when he hears a favourite female teacher's name.

When satisfied with his almost ten-year-old look
he sets off on his wheels with his bug container
towards logs covered in leaf mould.

Harmonious

He hummed as he blustered
heaved all his force
into the small metal organ,
a gasp in, a breath out,
a breath out, a gasp in
kisses of life for a pulse
a heartbeat
to awaken the melody.

After a decade of muteness
his diligence, his effort
answered by a splutter
a summer zephyr
through a wind chime
the song of the first cuckoo.
His tune earning him possibilities.

Balloon in the Breeze

Without effort, he slides down the zip-wire,
his school pals chant his name
a throb of rhythm, cheer,
football supporters in training,
who root for their favourite player:
a mantra for success.
Within the safety-suit, he dangles,
a boy with bottle,
undefined by his disability
for a moment

a balloon in the breeze.

What Really Gets to Me

Mostly, I hear beyond the lack of subtleties of spoken word
our simple but effective exchanges enough to grasp
the gist of what we mean.

I see past the fact that your legs can't walk like mine,
instead I appreciate your gifts
your sense of comedy, your engaging nature.

You guide me to places I have never journeyed
nor would, were it not for you.
What really gets to me are parents who make their children

stand still when they run around in circles being aeroplanes
or dragons, or show impatience when they ask
too many 'why' questions, or talk incessantly.

This really gets to me.

Spillweir 4 (Getting Him into Secondary School)

She plunges headfirst into the flowing-frenzy
drenched in the deluge of reports, opinions.
Her spirit fragments

as she is swept crazily out of control
a sinking bouquet she verges towards muddy banks,
struggles to avoid being submerged,

drowned by the flow, the energy soak-away-force
from those in power, the weight. She slips,
hangs on by a reed to her beliefs, dredges up her

hopes, opens airways to regain her breath
reaches home on garland floats
her lifebuoy of strength and drive.

Optimism

How agreeable it is to stroll through this sleepy place
dressed in sandals, a cotton dress,
bug-hunting with my Grandson.

The trowel engrossed in last autumn's dried leaves
finds little life for his pot. Instead, we discover
around the bottom of an ash

a choir of open-mouthed crimson lips,
their refrain illuminates the shadows
of the kneeling headstones.

We Sing

Sea-salty crisps
his addictive crystal
fizz on taste buds
after a flavour-famine,

mash and gravy
a feast of being able
to eat, to chew. Salmon, smoked,
torn off pieces, tiny,

digestible, evoke
a melody of flavour;
a chorus to show off
what he can now savour.

Our Winner

Drawn to the screen
by the theme tune's rhythm
swirling exotic organisms
take to the floor.
Disregarded,
he shows curiosity
in the beards and moustaches
of their partners,
a desire to copy them
when he is older.
His palms meet the challenge of clapping
at the close of each pair's performance
as though he is top of the leader-board
or the winner
of the much sought after
glitter ball.

Festival-goer

A ballyhoo of music, a flutter of silk flags,
gaily dressed crowds, birds-of-paradise

who carry backpacks full of good humour, fun.
Freedom calls out, his journey's begun

as he wanders at will, collects hellos
and smiles from other festival-goers.

He makes his own way to the transformation station,
where glitter, face paints, more smiles await him.

Spinning-top children circle music's beat
as he is danced in his wheelchair around

a fiesta of tapping fingers, the festival's feet,
until night wraps its sparkly cloak,

around a childhood almost complete.

This Space is Reserved for a Wheelchair

The Head of Play Parks

The man from the council sat on my couch, in response
to our request for equipment in parks round about.
He listened to suggestions to suit our child

whose legs would not bend into swings or slither down slides.
There was little for him to play on except the wet grass. He
smiled sympathetically and told us

*He would do his very best but it might require a bigger
spend than his budget would stretch.* We looked every day
and within three weeks or less in a nearby

park there appeared an accessible swing seat waiting for us.
This result was exciting, it made us feel heard and lo and
behold in another park eventually three more

swing seats appeared. Clearly not a one off, the man kept on
the case, he provided a roundabout for wheelchairs with room
for other children to sit, hang on to, or chase.

Paralympics July 2012

With an abracadabra we were welcomed across London's
coloured lines by fairy-godmother game makers
who waved wands of helpful smiles,

friendly words. Our difference blended into a
background of respect and foresight,
where disability sparkled and won trophies

a symbol of achievement for competitors
and supporters alike. Among our memories, a potential
prince in a wheelchair leapt

like a frog onto an escalator, his knack and know-how
amazed us with his adeptness. Another whose hands
appeared out of his shoulders

opened his purse, captivating us with an activity he'd
no need to rehearse. When midnight came, our emotions
elated, we returned homeward

Cinderellas from the ball, to a contradictory place where
our assistant to help us off the train had failed to appear:
sadly, there were still ugly sisters after all.

An Inconvenience

Many of them are dotted
around the town
silver doors labelled
with the blue badge sign
insides almost as sterile as
an operating room.
The main attraction
is to play with the tap
because the transfer
from wheelchair to toilet seat
is a big handicap
impossible without hoist
changing table or toilet seat
these accessible loos are only
useful for those who can stand
on two feet.

This Space is Reserved for a Wheelchair

or a large shopping trolley, a box on wheels,
a toddler in a pushchair or a passenger
who disregards the sign that reads,
This space is reserved for a wheelchair.

This space is reserved for a wheelchair.
or a traveller with a large rucksack,
a DIY enthusiast with shelves (flat pack)
covers the sign that declares,
This space is reserved for a wheelchair.

This space is reserved for a wheelchair.
or a dog who cannot read (his owner can),
a shopper laden with groceries in plastic bags
conceals the notice that demands,
This space is reserved for a wheelchair

This space is reserved for a wheelchair
so can we board this bus?
Sorry love says the driver *our policy
is first come first served,* to deny us
The space reserved for a wheelchair

A Prayer

Let there be taxi drivers who know how to assist my Grandson
and others with a disability; how to roll his wheelchair
as efficiently as a tea trolley into a taxi safely
without spilling sighs or swear words.

Let them not pass us down the rank as though we are
infectious in the hope there will be other drivers able to
take us, or tell us to get out at our request to strap him
in because they say they haven't been trained,
an excuse that's worn thin as ribbon.

Let there be smiles on their faces
kind words at each click
of the safety strap-downs at the front and back
of each wheel hook, a joke shared as the seat belt is adjusted,
the door firmly locked shut.

Amen

Swimming Pool blues

The first time I took my Grandson swimming
to the local pool, I suggested to the manager
it would be beneficial to create a facility
to make getting undressed and dressed stress-free

for those in a wheelchair or others with a disability.
For example, I added in my friendly way
(just a little a swagger in my voice),
a cubicle with a shower and a changing table
would be a nice, alongside the toilet and

all in the same place if given a choice.
She listened to my plan with a glazed look in her eyes,
then with a stubborn attitude, she declared with a smile
We don't get any wheelchair users coming to this pool.

.

Speaking Out

A hall dull as lamp-light
floors dusty, frayed at the edges
with a fringe of ancient gas fires
bags of forgotten stuff.

An odour of uncleaned toilets
linger around the helpers
pre-programmed to shout at the boys
to stand to attention or to shush,

apart from our boy who is obscured
by their outfits of ignorance,
lack of forethought. They avoid eye contact,
play non-inclusive games and sports,

keep him invisible, a ghost.
But I am forced to speak out,
explain my expectations about equality
then I shout louder than most.

Thanks also to;

All those professionals and others who have assisted in making life easier for my grandson and his family (too many to mention), ensuring that we have access to appropriate equipment; the NHS for their expertise, and Bristol City Council for funding house adaptions and carers etc.

Additionally, all the staff at Emersons Green Primary School for their ongoing and unwavering support. They have been brilliant in making sure my Grandson is moving towards better communication and have included him in everything all the able bodied children do. They really do understand and know how to implement inclusion.

Finally, to all the charities who have given or lent us equipment, or provided a service specifically for children like my Grandson, including Cerebral Palsy Plus and Music Space.

If you have not been mentioned in the poems, please don't be offended. We have appreciated everything to date you have done for us.

Cerebral Palsy Plus

Funds raised from the sale of this book will go to **Cerebral Palsy Plus,** a Bristol UK charity supporting and working with children and adults with cerebral palsy, along with their families and carers. The organisation aims to enhance the quality of life of those with cerebral palsy, enabling them to live as independently as possible, providing companionship for isolated disabled people in the community and direct support for families to help alleviate the pressures of caring for a family member with cerebral palsy at home.